Margaret
It was such a pleasure
meeting you! I pray God
Blessing on you!

Love Walk

The Christian's Responsibility to Love All People

LaMarcus A. Keys

renownpublishing

Renown Publishing
www.renownpublishing.com

Love Walk / LaMarcus A. Keys
ISBN: 978-1-952602-53-5

To my wife—Danielle Keys—for believing in me and being my biggest support and my best friend. Our journey together started more than twenty-six years ago, when we were two young teens full of faith, hope, and dreams and determined to set out on a journey to accomplish things that neither of us had ever experienced. What an awesome ride it has been, and I have enjoyed every minute of it with you! I am the man, the father, and the husband I am today because of you. You are my breath. I love you, babe, more than words can express. Thanks for just being you! You're perfect the way you are!

To my daughters—Jasmine, Jada, and Jordyn—for being my heartbeat. You three mean everything to me. You all inspire me to work harder and dream bigger. I do what I do to leave a legacy for you. You are smart, talented, and beautiful, and you love God! I aim daily to be an example of a godly and loving man like the ones you'll one day meet and marry to start families of your own. Out of all the titles and degrees given to me, the one that I'm really proud of is being called your Dad.

Lastly, in memory of my former pastor and mentor Apostle Frederick K. C. Price, who taught me how to walk by faith and not by sight. He taught me what it means to be a husband of integrity, a father of integrity, and a pastor of integrity. I don't know where I'd be today without his example and teachings. I know that in Heaven, he's receiving his well-deserved rest and rewards, and hopefully he can see the significant imprint that he left on my life. I never got the chance to tell him this personally, so I figured that I'd do the next best thing and tell the world and those I inspire about the man who inspired me.

CONTENTS

A New Commandment

Jesus said, "Let me give you a new command: Love one another. In the same way I loved you, you love one another. This is how everyone will recognize that you are my disciples—when they see the love you have for each other" (John 13:34–35 MSG). If Jesus gives you instructions, don't you think that it would be wise to follow them? Who would ignore the instructions of Jesus? A lot of people do so every day.

Jesus said that people would recognize us as His followers by the love we share with one another. Love isn't predicated upon someone being deserving or not, and it's not motivated by feelings.

Have you noticed how we, as the body of Christ, sometimes come across as the most unloving people? It can often appear that the world is more loving than the church, especially when people come through our doors and find a group that has huddled itself together to judge and whisper about others. Making the choice not to walk in love can leave a lasting negative stain on our witness for Christ.

The church is like a hospital. Healthy people don't go to the hospital unless they're working or visiting, but sick people come to the hospital to get better. Now imagine if all the healthy people frowned at the sick and said, "What are they doing here? Weren't they just here last week? Why are they here again?"

That should never be the case. The church should be a place where people can come in and feel the love of God in a way they have never experienced before. In some cases, we're the only model of God they're going to see before they see God for themselves. As a practical strategy at our church, Life of Victory Worship Center, we take the time to greet people, hug them if that's what they need or want, love on them, and let them know that they are welcome. This cultivates an environment of great love.

In this book, we're going to look at this subject from a biblical standpoint and uncover what it means to have the great responsibility of exemplifying the love of God to everybody we meet. We may not have everything together, but that shouldn't stop us from trying to perfect our love walk.

We need to get this right if we want to love God's way. That's what this book is all about, so let's take this journey of love together!

CHAPTER ONE

Love for the World to See

As the Father loved Me, I also have loved you; abide in My love. If you keep My commandments, you will abide in My love, just as I have kept My Father's commandments and abide in His love.

These things I have spoken to you, that My joy may remain in you, and that your joy may be full. This is My commandment, that you love one another as I have loved you.
—John 15:9–12 (NKJV)

God has put a big emphasis on love, and if you want to keep His commandments, you have to love. You can't circumvent love in pursuit of everything else. You have to make sure that you're walking in love. The way God loves us, the way Christ loves us, is the same type of love we need to share with others around us. It's a command, not a suggestion.

You have to love that person who cuts you off on the freeway. You have to love the person who annoys you. You have to love the person who mistreats you. You have to love the person who hates you. I'm not talking about liking those people. I'm talking about loving them.

It's ironic that we so easily seek God for better relationships, to know His purpose and plan for our lives, and for our needs to be met and desires to be fulfilled, yet we lack in love for others, especially our enemies. If love is big enough and important enough for Christ to address it as the greatest commandment, then it must be key to everything.

What Love Is

There are four different types of love in the Greek language:[1]

Eros: romantic love
Philia: friendship
Storge: affection
Agape: unconditional love

Each of these types of love can be godly and healthy, but the type that gets the most emphasis in the Bible is *agape* love, which is unconditional.

Unconditional Love

Imagine if God were moody and finicky like us and shared His love based on how good we are. Most of us would never experience the love of God!

Instead, God gave His Son unconditionally. The Bible says that the greatest love is to lay down your life for a friend (John 15:13). If you think about it, Christ went beyond that when He laid down His life for those who opposed Him. Romans 5:8 says, "God demonstrates His own love toward us, in that while we were still sinners, Christ died for us" (NKJV).

Jesus was persecuted by people whom we would call "haters" today. He had an opportunity to take down all those jokers while on the cross, but the love in Him spoke up. He responded, "Father, forgive them, because they don't know what they are doing" (Luke 23:34 NCV).

Likewise, our love toward other people shouldn't be based on whether those we love receive and accept us, but rather on the commandment Christ gave us. In fact, the Bible lets us know that if people oppose us when we're doing right, then God gets involved in our affairs and those people have to deal with Him (Romans 12:17–19). It's not up to us to take "an eye for an eye, and a tooth for a tooth" (Matthew 5:38–42 NCV). We have to love.

We may think that we're walking in love, but we're not really walking in the *right* love, in *agape* love. Sometimes we say that we're walking in love, but in reality, we're walking in "like." Our love may be conditional, based on how people treat us or if we approve of how they're living. The moment things aren't going our way with people, we cast them aside because we don't like them anymore.

This type of conditional love is *philia* love. It's the kind of love we give our friends. When they aren't our friends anymore, we lose that *philia* love we had for them. *Agape* love, the one we're emphasizing, is the one Christ requires us to demonstrate. It's unconditional, meaning that no matter what people do to us, our responsibility is always to love them as Christ loves us.

First Corinthians 13:4–7 (NCV) gives us the biblical definition of love:

> *Love is patient and kind. Love is not jealous, it does not brag, and it is not proud. Love is not rude, is not selfish, and does not get upset with others. Love does not count up wrongs that have been done. Love takes no pleasure in evil but rejoices over the truth. Love patiently accepts all things. It always trusts, always hopes, and always endures.*

Love doesn't say, "I have to give this person a piece of my mind because he annoys and frustrates me." If you're operating in love, then you must have patience and kindness toward other people. If you don't, then you're not walking in God's kind of love.

No Ill Will

There were instances in my past when I felt a sense of relief when something bad happened to somebody who did me wrong. I thought, *"See, that's what you get!"*

I was happy that something terrible was happening, because I thought it was deserved, but that's not love. We shouldn't rejoice in evil or when negative things happen to people who treated us poorly, because love wishes even our enemies well and prays that good things will happen to them (Matthew 5:44).

If you say that you love people and then you talk unkindly about them behind their backs, that's not God's kind of love. You can't both love people and wish evil upon them. When it comes to love, we can't allow ourselves to be entrenched in bitterness, detest people, or walk in offense (Psalms 119:165). These attitudes are usually byproducts of unforgiveness, which itself is a byproduct of hurt. If you don't deal with unforgiveness, then it grows into an attitude of taking offense. God says that if you want Him to forgive you, you first have to forgive other people (Matthew 6:14–15).

If love is guarding your heart and your lifestyle, it will protect you from getting offended. It's entirely possible for us not to allow offense into our hearts. Those of us who have been touched by God's unconditional love shouldn't allow our love to be clouded by resentment toward people who wrong us.

People are going to mistreat you and say negative things about you. Guess what. Your responsibility as a minister of reconciliation is to love them anyway (2 Corinthians 5:18–19).

We're All Part of the Same Body

Romans 12:4–5 (NKJV) says this:

> *For as we have many members in one body, but all the members do not have the same function, so we, being many, are one body in Christ, and individually members of one another.*

God looks at us as a complete body of Christ. Even though we have local churches, we're still collectively the body of Christ. You may be a finger, a toe, a knee, a hair strand, or an ear, but whatever part you are, you're a member of the body. We're all needed to make the body whole and complete.

At Odds with One Another

Since God views us as one body, it must look silly to Him when we're at odds with each other. Imagine that I'm walking down the street, just chilling and enjoying the sunshine, and then I slap myself in the head. What would you think if you saw that? It would be comical, right?

You would be confused and come over to me. You would ask me, "Pastor, is everything okay?"

I would reply (while continuing to smack my head over and over), "Yeah, everything is fine. It's just that my hand is upset with my head right now. When I was getting dressed this morning, my hand got jealous that my head had more time in the mirror than my hand did. As a result, they don't want to be around each other anymore."

You would look at that scenario and think, *"Come on, dude, something isn't right. You may want to get that looked at. Go to the doctor and get some meds."*

I believe that's what it looks like from God's viewpoint when we're at odds with each other and fighting with each other instead of walking in love, because God sees us as one body. Jesus died—was murdered, really—for the sake of His children being as one. There's nothing people can do to you that would make it right for you not to love them. Look at what people did to Christ.

When was the last time somebody spat on you?

When was the last time somebody beat you for false claims?

When was the last time you were arrested when you did nothing wrong?

The Bible tells us that Christ was beaten so badly that He was beyond human recognition (Isaiah 52:14). He was then mocked and made to carry His cross (Matthew 27:27–31; John 19:17). Then He was put on that cross and crucified (Matthew 27:35, 45–50). People did all these things to Jesus, and He didn't seek revenge. His boys (the disciples) were ready to defend Him, but Christ told them to stop (John 18:10–11). If Christ has shown you how to love properly despite how He was persecuted, then whatever you're facing, you can overcome it and love properly as He did.

No Jealousy

If God sees us as one body, it doesn't make sense to compete with each other. That's why I shouldn't be jealous or envious. The Bible says that we are to esteem others greater than ourselves (Philippians 2:3).

My hand is happy when my head is blessed. Do you know why? If my head is blessed, then my hand will be blessed. My hand isn't mad when my butt gets to sit in a new car. No, my hand is excited, too, because they both get to enjoy the new car.

The Bible tells us to "rejoice with those who rejoice" (Romans 12:15 NKJV). We should be excited for one another. We should be thinking of others more than ourselves. I want you to be blessed, because if you're blessed, it's a sign that God shows no favoritism. What He did for you He can do for me. There's no hating here; there's no jealousy here. But if you're not walking in love, you open the door for all of those negative thoughts and emotions to enter.

Unprotected

Some of the bad things we encounter are not a direct product of Satan, but rather a byproduct of doors we've left open in our lives because of our choices.

Imagine if I were leaving my house and chose not to secure it properly and turn on the alarm. Instead, I opened the doors wide and left the windows open. Then I put up yard signs saying how much valuable stuff I had in the house, like a brand-new sixty-inch TV and a nice car in the garage. To top it all off, I left a sticky note saying, "By the way, I won't be home from 8 a.m. to 5 p.m., and I have no dog." If a thief came in and stole some things, it wouldn't be entirely his own idea. I left my property unprotected and essentially invited the thief into my house.

When we choose not to walk in love toward each other, we leave ourselves unprotected and open for the enemy to come into our lives.

Working on Love

Before I got married, I sat down with some guys who gave me great wisdom in terms of how to have a successful marriage.

They asked, "How do you spell *marriage*?"

I knew that one. I thought, *"I'm going to pass this test."*

So I started out, "M. A. R.—"

They didn't even let me finish. They said, "No. You spell it: W. O. R. K."

You have to work at marriage. You have to give and sacrifice willingly, and it will be hard. If you go into it with that attitude, and the other person goes into it with the same attitude, you have the foundation for a great marriage. On the other hand, if you have two people joining together who think that it's their way or the highway, the marriage will not be successful.

Why not? Because it will be like two bulls locking horns. Somebody has to yield, to take the first step, to be the bigger person and say, "No, I'm going to sacrifice here."

Love—in all contexts—requires work, but if you stick with it, the benefits are phenomenal.

Walking in Love Through Christ

Is walking in love easy? No. Can it be difficult? Yes. Can you do it? Absolutely!

Sometimes in boxing competitions, you see the verse Philippians 4:13—"I can do all things through Christ, because he gives me strength" (NCV)—written on the boxers' shorts, on their jerseys, or on their robes before they come out.

Well, when it comes to obeying the Word of God, you can do anything through Christ, who strengthens you.

When it comes to loving people who seem unlovable, you can do anything through Christ, who strengthens you.

This verse isn't talking about an athletic event; it's talking about living out the Word of God. You *can* do it, and you *have* to do it.

Lifestyle of a Believer

You have to control yourself. The Bible tells us that "we walk by faith, not by sight" (2 Corinthians 5:7 NKJV). See, faith isn't just something you exercise when you want something. It's the lifestyle of a believer.

You have to walk by faith when it comes to loving others. You have to walk by faith when it comes to forgiving people. Your flesh will tell you, "No!" Satan will try to replay in your head all of the wrongs that people have committed against you. You will hear every negative conversation again and again. But then, as the Bible says, you have to subject yourself to the Word (1 Corinthians 9:27). You have to make yourself comply with Scripture.

I'm not talking to your mind, your will, your emotions, or your body. I'm talking to your heart. It's a heart transformation that enables you to walk in love. You can't check in with your mind or your emotions on this. Those parts of you are like amusement park rides: they go up and down and all around. They're all over the place. With your heart, you have to command yourself to walk in love.

Seven Responsibilities

We have seven responsibilities that demonstrate love for each other:

1. Pray for one another.
2. Lend and provide for one another.
3. Be sensitive to each other's needs.
4. Give preference to one another.
5. Have no jealousy.
6. Forgive one another.
7. Build each other up.

We will dive into each of these specific responsibilities more in the following chapter, but know this: when we don't feel like loving others, we have to do it anyway out of obedience to God. Furthermore, the love we demonstrate isn't just for us; it's so that everyone around us might see and experience the love of God.

For All to See

A new commandment I give to you, that you love one another; as I have loved you, that you also love one another. By this all will know that you are My disciples, if you have love for one another.

—John 13:34–35 (NKJV)

The love Jesus commands us to walk in isn't just for our benefit; it's also for the benefit of the people watching us. You walking in love toward me, and I toward you, is a lot bigger and more important than just you and I. Our love impacts hundreds, even thousands, of people.

Did you know that if you're not walking in love, it can hinder your witness? Not only can it hinder your witness, but it can also be a black eye for the body of Christ. I've run into people who say that they're fed up with church. They say that church is phony, that people are acting fake behind those doors. We aren't showing love toward one another or the world around us.

My heart's position is this: I'm walking in this love thing so completely that if a night worker were to come into service on a Sunday morning, I would want to give her a seat in the front row instead of trying to hide her in the back out of shame or disgust. I wouldn't want anybody staring at her with judgment. I would want her to have the opportunity to experience the true love of God.

Catching Fish

Our responsibility as believers isn't to clean the fish, but to catch the fish. If we catch the fish, Holy Spirit will clean the fish. Some of us try to clean before we catch, but if you've ever been fishing, you know that you can never catch a clean fish. It would be amazing if you could, because I don't like the scaling or the gutting; it's nasty business. But in order to enjoy the fish, you have to catch it in its current condition.

Our responsibility is to reel people in with love. Once we get them in, Holy Spirit will do the rest. Holy Spirit is still working on you and me, after all. We aren't perfect; we aren't without fault. Our only responsibility is to get people into an environment where they can experience the love of God without condemnation. They can come and receive whatever God has for them without the hurdle of other people looking at them like they're unworthy.

Shallow Appearance

I remember attending a church with strict rules when I was younger. Some of those rules were that women weren't allowed to wear open-toed shoes or red nail polish. Women always had to be in dresses, and those dresses needed to be below the knee. No high heels, lipstick, or big earrings were allowed. There were a lot of rules in place that addressed the outward appearance. I can only imagine how many fish were never caught because they didn't fit the mold created by human expectations. Perhaps as a result, they never got a chance to experience what it meant to be truly loved.

I also remember that when I was a kid, there was one church with some teenagers who got pregnant. I don't endorse their behavior at all, but this particular church kicked them out. I didn't know a lot then, but I knew that they were my peers. I saw them with tearful eyes, beating themselves up but having no place to go.

I thought to myself, *"Man, church is the place they should be to receive information and know how to go on and live prosperous lives."* I figured that they had to deal with their mistakes for the rest of their lives, so the important thing was to help them get healed and be whole. Instead, they got booted out.

Of course, the kids got older and had animosity toward the church, painting the entire body of Christ with a single, wide brush. The reality is that when someone in the church makes a mistake, people often use the biggest brush available and convince themselves that everyone in the body of Christ is like that.

This is why the Bible says that walking in love toward one another lets the world know that we are disciples of Christ. A lack of love impacts our witness and can keep people from coming to Christ. Just as Christ, with open arms, receives individuals who have made mistakes, you and me included, we have to extend the same love toward other people.

One time when I wore jeans, somebody came up to me and remarked, "Oh, you're supposed to be a minister?"

I said, "Yes, ma'am."

The woman said, "Ministers aren't supposed to wear jeans!"

She threw condemnation all over me, and I have to admit that I was confused when I got through talking with her. Was I doing something wrong?

It wasn't about my lifestyle. It wasn't about my relationship with God. It was about my physical appearance.

Some people have the walk down and have the talk down but are as mean as they come. They are full of hatred, envy, and jealousy, but they look the part of the Christian. They know how to clap on beat and shout on cue when the music is good.

I'm interested in love. I'm interested in your relationship with God. I'm interested in you being everything God has called you to be. I'm interested in you discovering the purpose God has for your life, walking out the Word of God, and experiencing the full manifestation of His covenant promises.

I'm after your heart. God will take care of everything on the outside. It's important for me to walk in love so that you can see it.

Take Off the Mask

I've heard it said that Sundays are the equivalent of October 31. Do you know what happens on that day? People wear masks.

We come into church with masks on, looking the part, trying to make people think that we're something. But underneath the masks, we're all messed up.

Take the mask off. I want your heart. I'm out to influence your lifestyle. No more faking. Be who God called you to be and experience everything God wants you to experience.

Haters will be haters. People will talk about you and treat you poorly, but getting back at them isn't worth sacrificing your relationship with God. You have to be committed to this love walk.

Victory Declared

God won't let something happen to us that we can't handle. In every temptation, He gives us a way of escape

(1 Corinthians 10:13). If somebody treats you badly, it's already been seen by God and allowed by God, and victory has already come as a result of it. God won't allow you to go through something you can't bear. It may be tough, and our difficult circumstances may differ, but whatever each of us goes through, God has preordained victory.

You are called to walk out the Word. You can trust God, and you need to do what He tells you to do. You have to love—there's no choice! It's a responsibility. If you rely on God without wavering and love as He calls you to love, you will enjoy everything He says you can have in His Word.

WORKBOOK

Chapter One Questions

Question: Have you ever felt like you weren't good enough to be a part of the church or that members of a church didn't accept you? If so, how does that impact how you treat others in and outside of the church? If not, how can you grow to a place of empathy for those who may feel like they don't belong in the church?

_____

_____

_____

_____

_____

_____

_____

_____

_____

Question: Which do you think you value more: the ideologies of your church and maintaining certain behaviors or showing people God's love? Do you find it difficult to love those whose lifestyle you don't agree with? Why do you think that is? What steps can you take to walk in love that more fully reflects God's unconditional love?

_____

_____

_____

_____

_____

_____

_____

_____

_____

Action: Choose someone in your life who would benefit from an act of kindness and do something for that person that conveys God's unconditional love without ulterior motives. Make it something practical and meaningful.

Chapter One Notes

_____

_____

_____

_____

_____

_____

_____

_____

_____

_____

_____

_____

_____

_____

_____

_____

_____

_____

_____

_____

_____

_____

_____

CHAPTER TWO

Seven Responsibilities of Love

As the Father loved Me, I also have loved you; abide in My love. If you keep My commandments, you will abide in My love, just as I have kept My Father's commandments and abide in His love.

These things I have spoken to you, that My joy may remain in you, and that your joy may be full. This is My commandment, that you love one another as I have loved you.
—John 15:9–12 *(NKJV)*

God has given us a responsibility to love. His Word is clear: love isn't an option. You don't have a right to decide whether or not you will love someone. Once this truth is settled in your heart, all that's left is to get a clear understanding of what it means to love. How does God define love?

First Corinthians 13:4–7 (NCV) gives us the biblical definition of love:

Love is patient and kind. Love is not jealous, it does not brag, and it is not proud. Love is not rude, is not selfish, and does not get upset with others. Love does not count up wrongs that have been done. Love takes no pleasure in evil but rejoices over the truth. Love patiently accepts all things. It always trusts, always hopes, and always endures.

God desires us, as the church, to foster and provide an environment of love. We are to be a place where anyone can come. People who come to church may have their guard up. They may be broken and bruised and have a hard time trusting. If we aren't filled with love, we will cause further damage and maybe even drive them away.

Now that we know what God's definition of love is, we can begin to live out the commandment to love. We're going to look at seven ways the Bible tells us to walk in love. This will give us a clear path to follow.

Pray for One Another

Since the day we heard these things about you, we have continued praying for you. This is what we pray: that God will make you completely sure of what he wants by giving you all the wisdom and spiritual understanding you need....
—Colossians 1:9 (ERV)

We are to pray for one another—not gossip about each other or judge each other, but pray. If you hear that somebody has sinned, your responsibility is to restore that person, not sit around and talk about him or her. There's a time and place for confronting people about their sin, but when we do, the purpose is to build them up and edify them, not to embarrass them, criticize them, or tear them down with harsh judgment.

If people know that they did something wrong, our right response is to forgive and restore them, not to get on a hotline and spread the news. You can be just as guilty by association, scooting your chair in closer to "get the tea" or hear the gossip. Instead, you should say, "What's the purpose of this conversation?" Be the one to hold up a standard. Don't allow the influence of someone else to cause you to ignore what the Word of God says about your responsibility to love.

I remember being in a difficult job situation years ago. No matter how hard I worked, management was set against me. No matter how much respect I showed, they continued to remove opportunities from me. I was so frustrated, and at times I wanted to leave the company. But whenever I asked God if I could leave, I never got the release. So I continued to do what the Word of God instructed me to do, which was to work "as to the Lord and not to men" (Colossians 3:23 NKJV). I still showed up every day with the right heart, the right mind, the right words, and the right work ethic, doing my job as if I were working for God Himself.

In addition, on my way to work every morning, I prayed for my management team, that their eyes would be opened to God's truth and that the opportunity to accept Him into their lives would be possible. I prayed for their well-being and their success. Mind you, this is when I was in the thick of things and knew that they were set against me. Why did I do this? Because I love God and God loves them.

There may be some people in your life who have done you wrong, maybe said horrible things about you or harmed you with their actions. I encourage you to walk in love toward them by praying for them. Jesus did this for those who put Him on the cross, so let's extend this love by praying for one another.

Lend to and Provide for One Another

When I'm out and about, sometimes a homeless person approaches me for money. In those situations, some may say, "Man, I'm not giving these jokers anything. They'd better go out and get a job. The nerve of them! All they'll do is smoke or drink my money away." You may have similar thoughts, and you may be right. However, these instances should be viewed as opportunities to be a witness for Christ through acts of kindness and love.

On countless occasions when I'm at a gas station, someone approaches me. At that point, I'm ready to go on my way, and my inclination is to leave or to be suspicious. My first thought is: *"Get away from me, please and thank you."* That's what I want to say, but when I identify it as an opportunity to witness to someone, I say, "I sure do have money for you!"

I actually keep pocket change in my car for this exact purpose, and when I have a business card for our church, I give that as well. As I pull out the money, I say, "First, let me ask you: do you know Christ as your Lord and personal Savior?" Whether or not the person does, I offer to pray for him, right then and there.

Then I'll say, "God bless you, brother. Here's the money and a card for my church. If you don't go there, I hope you'll go somewhere else the Word of God is taught. Welcome to the Kingdom." Now that's an inexpensive transaction: a small seed given in exchange for a life brought into God's kingdom.

Jesus said, "If a person asks you for something, give it to him. Don't refuse to give to someone who wants to borrow from you" (Matthew 5:42 NCV). The next time you see a homeless person outside of a market, will you roll up your windows and lock your doors, or will you welcome the request for help? This is an opportunity to witness! This person asked you for something, so you can ask for something, too, right?

Once I saw a homeless man digging through some trash near my car. My family was in the car when he approached me. I rolled down my window, and my baby said, "I know it's about to go down again, and daddy's about to pray for him!"

"Excuse me, sir. Do you have any money?" he asked.

"I sure do! Give me a second." As I reached over to grab my money, I asked, "Do you know Christ as your Lord and Savior?"

As I sat there, the man started crying. He said, "I can't do this. I have to go."

Immediately, I replied, "No, come back over here. God loves you. I love you. God has a purpose and a plan for your life. Do you mind if I pray for you?"

He said, "Sure," and stuck his worn hands into my car.

I grabbed his hands and led him to Christ, and then I gave him the money. When he walked away, my baby said, "Dad, you made that man cry!" Well, I didn't make him cry; he was just excited to accept Christ into his life.

Opportunities to help are all around us. What an individual does with the money you give is between that person and God.

Whatever you sow, you reap. If you give, "it will be given to you" (Luke 6:38 NKJV). How many opportunities do we pass up each day? You don't have to wait to hear from God. The Bible already tells us to give. I also believe that this is an example of an area of stewardship. God blesses you to bless others. He says that if you're "faithful over a few things, [He] will make you ruler over many things" (Matthew 25:23 NKJV). If you want to have a financial breakthrough, be obedient and open with the finances God has blessed you with. God has given freely to you, so give freely to others (Matthew 10:8).

The Brotherhood

The early church took from their increase and distributed among the saints. "They had all things in common," and no one lacked anything he needed (Acts 4:32–35 NKJV).

Romans 12:13 describes love as "distributing to the needs of the saints, given to hospitality" (NKJV). The body of Christ should look out for one another, circulating our dollars, and not depend on the world's system to support us.

Our dollars have a voice. If we become a brotherhood, locking hands with one another so no one is lacking or insufficient, how powerful could we be? How much more effective could we be in expanding God's kingdom? We should be able to believe in and live out the Word of God to the point where we don't have insecurities about going up to a fellow Christian and asking for help. It requires all of us to love as we have been loved, without reservation or restraint.

Be Sensitive to One Another's Needs

There's a mandate for believers to walk in love. We have the responsibility to love all people, even those who offend us. News flash: it isn't all about you. Romans 12:15 says, "Rejoice with those who rejoice, and weep with those who weep" (NKJV). We need to be sensitive to the needs of those around us.

Sometimes we can be insensitive to what's going on in other people's lives. Maybe we feel that they should get over it or that they deserve their misfortune, but our responsibility is to be considerate of their needs. We need to be sensitive to where other people are in life, even if it's not where we are.

I'm a Fire Chaplain, and being part of this community has shown me the importance of being sensitive to the particular moment and stage of each person's life. A chaplain usually shows up in the darkest, most difficult moments of people's lives. I was taught that being a chaplain requires you to operate in the "ministry of presence." It's not about having all the answers or solving all the problems; it's about being there for others during hard times and staying sensitive to their needs. This is a demonstration of God's love.

Give Preference to One Another

Love is intentional. It doesn't require a thrill. As a matter of fact, when the thrill isn't there, that's when true *agape* love kicks in and is revealed. It's in the moments when you don't feel the emotion of love that unconditional love has to work extra hard. Philippians 2:1–4 (NKJV) says:

> *Therefore if there is any consolation in Christ, if any comfort of love, if any fellowship of the Spirit, if any affection and mercy, fulfill my joy by being like-minded, having the same love, being of one accord, of one mind. Let nothing be done through selfish ambition or conceit, but in lowliness of mind let each esteem others better than himself. Let each of you look out not only for his own interests, but also for the interests of others.*

What does it mean to esteem others better than yourself? I think it looks something like this: If you hear that Best Buy has a huge sale on large-screen TVs, you might race over there to get one before they sell out. You might stand in line for hours. Then you hear that there's only one TV left. You look at the person beside you, knowing that he wants the TV, too. Do you know what love would do? It would say, "I see that you really want this. You can go ahead and have it." That's an example of esteeming others better than yourself and looking out for others' interests more than your own.

Esteeming others can also mean letting people skip in front of you at the grocery store, giving people the benefit of the doubt, and turning the other cheek. These are just daily practical examples. If it's hard to put others before yourself in small, day-to-day things, it will be even more difficult to do so when it comes to spiritual matters.

No Jealousy

Love is patient and kind. Love is not jealous, it does not brag, and it is not proud. Love is not rude, is not selfish, and does not get upset with others. Love does not count up wrongs that have been done. Love takes no pleasure in evil but rejoices over the truth. Love patiently accepts all things. It always trusts, always hopes, and always endures.
—1 Corinthians 13:4–7 *(NCV)*

Remember that this is God's definition of love. When He tells us to love other people as He loves us, this is how we're supposed to love them. Among other things, walking in love includes not being *jealous*, or "hostile towards a rival or one believed to enjoy an advantage."[2] People walking in jealousy have issues with others who appear to be doing better than they are. A modern term for this sort of person is a "hater."

Do you have a problem with people when you see that they got a new pair of shoes or your dream car? It bothers you because you want what someone else has. A jealous person doesn't believe that there's enough to go around. Are you jealous when someone else gets the job you wanted or when someone gets pregnant while you continue to struggle with infertility?

If you find yourself feeling jealous, it may be because you aren't operating in faith and love. You need to understand that there's no insufficiency with God. He has everything. He has exactly what you desire in His hands.

Romans 13:13–14 says, "Let us walk properly, as in the day, not in revelry and drunkenness, not in lewdness and lust, not in strife and envy. But put on the Lord Jesus Christ, and make no provision for the flesh, to fulfill its lusts" (NKJV). These verses categorize envy as the lust of the flesh.

James 3:14–16 (NCV) says:

> But if you are selfish and have bitter jealousy in your hearts, do not brag. Your bragging is a lie that hides the truth. That kind of "wisdom" does not come from God but from the world. It is not spiritual; it is from the devil. Where jealousy and selfishness are, there will be confusion and every kind of evil.

If you're jealous and have bitter selfishness in your heart, don't brag about how much you love God and want to please Him and do His will, because your boasting will be inaccurate. If you're not fulfilling His commandments, then you're bragging about a God you're not serving.

How many adults still like to eat baby food? You used to enjoy it, but you don't anymore because you have outgrown it. Titus 3:3 says, "For we ourselves were also once foolish, disobedient, deceived, serving various lusts and pleasures, living in malice and envy, hateful and hating one another" (NKJV).

When we talk about the responsibility to love, it isn't baby food; it's the fruit of a mature believer. Walking in envy is foolish. It's possible that you are confessing that God will deliver you, but you're still stuck in bondage because you don't truly believe what you're saying or because your actions don't agree with your confession. If you say that you believe in God, your lifestyle needs to be in agreement with God's Word.

Perhaps the enemy is still beating you down because you're still participating in his extracurricular activities. How can you expect God to deliver you when you're operating in jealousy and envy? We are to "be doers of the word, and not hearers only" (James 1:22 NKJV). Some hear the Word but don't do anything with it. God can't bless you when you refuse to follow His instructions and continue to walk in jealousy.

I've discovered two practical methods for removing jealousy from your life:

1. When you're tempted to be jealous, immediately rebuke the spirit of jealousy and its attack on your mind, emotions, and life (2 Corinthians 10:5). Don't be passive and let it torment you. Be aggressive and drive it away through and by the power of Holy Spirit, in Jesus' name!

2. Do the opposite of what jealousy is suggesting to you. Find a way to demonstrate a gesture of

kindness. Pray for the person whom the devil is trying to get you to be jealous of.

Forgive One Another

Then Peter came to Him and said, "Lord, how often shall my brother sin against me, and I forgive him? Up to seven times?"

Jesus said to him, "I do not say to you, up to seven times, but up to seventy times seven."
—Matthew 18:21–22 *(NKJV)*

Don't be surprised if you feel challenged after reading these verses. God has planted the seed of love in your heart, and then Satan comes along and tries to take it away. He may do that by bringing someone into your life who hurts you or brings disappointment, testing your love walk.

In the scripture above, I actually think that Peter was being generous. He was already giving a number that he felt was above and beyond what he should have to forgive.

How many times have people done something wrong to you? Some of us have allowed offense to take root in our hearts. This is a byproduct of not dealing with and getting rid of unforgiveness. First comes hurt, then unforgiveness, and then offense. Unforgiveness is like old food left in the fridge. Unless you remove the food from the fridge, mold will grow. Offense is old, moldy unforgiveness that hasn't been dealt with. When you continue to walk in unforgiveness, offense takes over. As a believer, you have to guard your heart against offense.

When was the last time somebody hurt you? Was that person a repeat offender? Did you forgive him or her?

Have you ever tried to talk to somebody who has been offended? It's like talking to a brick wall. If you aren't careful, you'll realize that you're also getting offended. It's rubbing off on you. That's how strong the spirit of offense is.

God doesn't put a limit on how many times we are to forgive someone. We can operate in wisdom and still offer forgiveness. The Bible tells us to bless those who hurt us and do good to those who do wrong to us (Matthew 5:44). That's our responsibility.

Jesus said, "I tell you not to resist an evil person. But whoever slaps you on your right cheek, turn the other to him also" (Matthew 5:39 NKJV). Before you get upset with me, I want you to remember who said this. Jesus made this statement. Was Jesus ever beaten or slapped? What did He do? He forgave those who hurt and insulted Him. He didn't even mutter a response. That's what it looks like to turn the other cheek. This is the place of love where He wants us to live. If Christ could endure all that He went through and still forgive, you can as well.

Ephesians 4:32 says, "And be kind to one another, tenderhearted, forgiving one another, even as God in Christ forgave you" (NKJV). When you understand that love serves, you will look for an opportunity to out-serve the other person, not for what you can get out of it but because of your responsibility to love.

Let God Heal You

God wants to heal our hearts. There are a lot of scars that you can't see. People can have smiles on their faces, and their lives may look fine from the outside, but they're bleeding and hurting on the inside. It's necessary to let God heal you, because you can't love the way you're supposed to love until He does.

A lot of people carry brokenness and hurt into their marriages. They can't be the wife or husband they're supposed to be, because they love from a position of hurt. Their hurt consumes all of their relationships, and they can't move forward.

If you don't address the hurt in your life, it will address you. Offense is so deceitful that you can harbor it and still think that everything is normal. You avoid people and cut them out of your life. You learn to live with it, but the Bible has commanded us not to be offended. That kind of mindset will handicap the love that God requires us to walk in.

You need to ask God to come in and mend your broken heart supernaturally. Then you will be able to love like you're supposed to love and forgive as Christ has called you to forgive.

Everything that you have faced, Christ faced and overcame. That's why He is our great example. In and through Christ, you will overcome every challenge. You don't have to worry about the people who did you wrong or think about how their lives are progressing, because God will take care of them and take care of you. You just do your part and extend love through forgiveness.

Build One Another Up

We then who are strong ought to bear with the scruples of the weak, and not to please ourselves. Let each of us please his neighbor for his good, leading to edification.
                    —Romans 15:1–2 (NKJV)

Let no corrupt word proceed out of your mouth, but what is good for necessary edification, that it may impart grace to the hearers. And do not grieve the Holy Spirit of God, by whom you were sealed for the day of redemption. Let all bitterness, wrath, anger, clamor, and evil speaking be put away from you, with all malice. And be kind to one another, tenderhearted, forgiving one another, even as God in Christ forgave you.
                    —Ephesians 4:29–32 (NKJV)

Sometimes words can be more detrimental than physical harm. Physical bruises heal, but words can leave us struggling mentally and emotionally for years. Because words are so powerful, Scripture tells us to watch what we say (Proverbs 18:21; James 3:1–12). Sometimes we get so angry that we try to find the most painful and poisonous words possible to launch at somebody, but that's not love.

We may have opinions about how we want other people to feel and what we want them to do, but we can't control their thoughts, feelings, or actions. We think that we need to stand up for ourselves and maybe even fight because we're afraid that people will continue to take advantage of us, but what does the Word tell us? Scripture tells us not to be rude, bitter, mad, or angry. Instead, we need to be kind and forgive as Christ forgave us (Ephesians 4:31–32). It takes a person of strength not to react with anger, but to respond in love.

The Word needs to govern our lives. If you want a car to run, you have to make sure that it has gas. If you want believers to flourish, you need to put the Word of God in them. If you choose to put anything into your life that's outside of the Word of God, it will impact the way you live. You will never live up to the full potential God has provided for you if you put inferior fuel into your life. However, if you put the Word of God into your life, it will help you to soar.

Watch Your Mouth

There's no place for gossip or slander in the love walk. We shouldn't be spreading rumors or speculating about other people's personal lives. Words are a gift. Before we say something, we need to examine whether it's truth or rumor. Will it defame the person we're about to talk about or lift that person up?

There's a time and place to address the sin of others, but you don't need to put people's lives on blast. What you can do is encourage people within the private confines of your relationship. Timothy wrote:

> *Remember this! In the last days there will be many troubles, because people will love themselves, love money, brag, and be proud. They will say evil things against others and will not obey their parents or be thankful or be the kind of people God wants. They will not love others, will refuse to forgive, will gossip, and will not control themselves. They will be cruel, will hate what is good, will turn against their friends, and will do foolish things without thinking. They will be conceited, will love pleasure instead of God, and will act as if they serve God but will not have his power. Stay away from those people.*
> *—2 Timothy 3:1–5 (NCV)*

> *Besides that, they learn to waste their time, going from house to house. And they not only waste their time but also begin to gossip and busy themselves with other people's lives, saying things they should not say.*
> *—1 Timothy 5:13 (NCV)*

We need to learn the art of being quiet. It takes great strength. If it's not edifying and it's not going to build the person up, don't say it.

Do Good

There are people who have put knives in my back (figuratively) by saying or doing hurtful things. As painful as that is, my responsibility is not to get back at them, fight them, or try to prove that they're wrong and I'm better than they are. As Ephesians 6:12 says, "We do not wrestle against flesh and blood" (NKJV). These people aren't my enemies. Just as God uses people, so does Satan.

If you want to defeat the enemy, then walk in love, because Satan isn't about love. God wants us to do good to people who have harmed us (Proverbs 25:21–22). That's what Christ did. His response was: "Father, forgive them" (Luke 23:34 NKJV).

We can love others with the love of Christ, but we need to make a commitment in our hearts to do it. God determines whether or not we love Him by the love we have for and demonstrate toward others. There's no other option.

Chapter Two Questions

Question: There are seven responsibilities of love a believer in Christ must demonstrate: pray for one another, lend and provide for one another, be sensitive to each other's needs, give preference to one another, have no jealousy, forgive one another, and build each other up. Which of these seven responsibilities is most apparent in your life? Which is least apparent in your life?

_____

_____

_____

_____

_____

_____

_____

_____

_____

_____

_____

Question: Is there any unforgiveness in your heart that's keeping you from moving forward in your love walk? How has this unforgiveness impacted your life? What would it look like for you to forgive that person? How would it change your life?

_____

_____

_____

_____

_____

_____

_____

_____

_____

_____

_____

Action: Choose the responsibility to demonstrate love that's least apparent in your life and ask God to show you how you can better display it. Write down the ideas that come to your mind. Pray that Holy Spirit will provide you with and show you opportunities to begin living this responsibility as an example of God's love to those around you. As the opportunities come, all you have to do is say *yes*!

Chapter Two Notes

_____

_____

_____

_____

_____

_____

_____

_____

_____

_____

_____

_____

_____

_____

_____

_____

_____

_____

_____

_____

_____

_____

_____

_____

CHAPTER THREE

Love That's Real

I remember when I gave my wife her first ring. It was a promise ring, and I thought that it was perfect. My pride was not baseless. I'd done all the research myself, picked it out, and spent significantly more than I'd planned to spend.

My wife didn't say anything against the ring when she accepted it, and I was soaring. However, my family was quick to bring to my attention that the quality of the ring was subpar. You could definitely see the diamonds, but only with several magnifying glasses. It didn't meet their standards for a ring of significance.

All of us like the real thing, something of value. We don't like anything fake. *Fake* means "not true, real, or genuine: counterfeit, sham; to alter, manipulate, or treat so as to give a spuriously genuine appearance; simulate; deceive."[3] For example, I prefer the taste of a real cola to the imitation called "dark soda." Fruit Loops are a great cereal, better than Circle O's. We all like the real thing.

Nobody likes a fake friend or a two-faced person, but sometimes we may find that we're the ones being fake and presenting something that we're not. Truth be told, that happens a lot in the church. We present an image for people to see, but our true character is totally different.

Jesus said, "I give you a new command: Love each other. You must love each other as I have loved you. All people will know that you are my followers if you love each other" (John 13:34–35 NCV). We are to love how Christ has loved us. People are going to judge us based on our love walk, so we need to represent the love of Christ well.

How many times have you talked to people who don't go to church and they've said that church people are fake or hypocritical? They are observing that what's coming out of our mouths doesn't match up with how we live our lives. Some people confess one thing, but their actions say something else. The way some believers are treating each other is creating a black eye for the body of Christ. Satan is rejoicing over this, but God is not!

Fifteen Characteristics of Love

Jesus told us that when we show love toward one another, other people will know that we are His followers. Sometimes people will base their decision to accept Christ on how we treat them or how they see us treating other people. Let's look again at the biblical definition of love:

Love is patient and kind. Love is not jealous, it does not brag, and it is not proud. Love is not rude, is not selfish, and does not get upset with others. Love does not count up wrongs that have been done. Love takes no pleasure in evil but rejoices over the truth. Love patiently accepts all things. It always trusts, always hopes, and always endures.
—1 Corinthians 13:4–7 *(NCV)*

This passage gives us fifteen requirements that must be met in order for us to fulfill the Bible's definition of love in our lives. This is what real love looks like. Is your love real or fake? The best way to uncover the fake is by learning what's real.

Love Is Patient

Patience is "the capacity to accept or tolerate delay, problems, or suffering without becoming annoyed or anxious."[4] Love is not short with people. If you're short with people and impatient, you aren't operating in God's kind of love.

Love isn't about how we feel or what we want to do. We may encounter people whom we want to be angry with, but we have to come back to spirituality and remind ourselves, *"Well, that's not exemplifying God's love toward this person."*

We are the gatekeepers of our own lives, including our thoughts, feelings, impulses, and actions (2 Corinthians 10:5). Just because you think something, feel something, or want to do something doesn't mean that you have to act on it. Through Christ, you have the ability to respond based on His Word and instructions. Even if your thoughts, feelings, and impulses are telling you to hate, you can still choose to respond with love. You are in control!

Jesus said, "You must love each other as I have loved you" (John 13:34 NCV). Christ is our greatest example, and He had the love and patience to endure persecution, ridicule, lies, false judgment, and crucifixion and still say, "Father, forgive them, for they do not know what they do" (Luke 23:34 NKJV). If Christ can have that attitude of love toward people who did Him the greatest harm possible, then you and I can surely handle whatever we're facing.

Love is patient. It handles delay, stress, and trouble without getting angry or upset. If anything in life gets you angry or upset, this is an indicator that your patience needs to be developed.

If you want bigger muscles, what do you have to do? You have to work out. You need to lift some weights to increase your muscle mass. Is that fun? No. It can be really painful, especially if you haven't done it in a while. What keeps you going back to that pain? You want the results of conditioning and getting to the size and strength you're trying to achieve. You endure the process of lifting weights so you can reach your goal.

God requires us to operate in patience, and the way to grow in patience is through trouble, trials, and pressure. Once you can go through difficulties without getting angry or upset, you know that your patience has developed in that area. That particular weight or exercise is no longer needed except for maintenance.

James 1:2–4 says, "Consider it a sheer gift, friends, when tests and challenges come at you from all sides. You know that under pressure, your faith-life is forced into the open and shows its true colors. So don't try to get out of anything prematurely. Let it do its work so you become mature and well-developed, not deficient in any way" (MSG).

If you ever get to a place where it's hard to love somebody, this indicates that your patience needs to be developed in that area. The only way patience can be developed is for you successfully to endure the challenge you're facing.

Love Is Kind

Real love means that you should care for other people more than yourself. This love causes us to put other people ahead of our own desires.

The golden rule is to treat others as you would have them treat you. How would you feel if a particular situation were reversed? We don't know where people are in their lives and what they're going through. An act of selfless kindness can transform someone's life.

There are times when I do a random act of kindness for someone and the benefits are amazing for everyone involved. It blesses the other person to receive something unexpected, and it blesses me to know that I helped someone out and was an extension of God's love in his or her life. Our church's Outreach Team (iReach) does this on occasion, whether it be giving out free water bottles at the beach, washing cars for free, cooking food for our neighboring businesses for free, or giving out free meals for Thanksgiving. There's something powerful and long-lasting, even eternal, about showing God's love through kindness.

Love Is Not Jealous

As we talked about in the previous chapter, avoiding jealousy is one of the responsibilities of a believer walking in love. It's also a characteristic of biblical love. Avoiding jealousy means that we don't hate people because they have what we want. There's never a reason for us, as God's children, to be jealous. We don't need to be jealous of people's possessions, careers, or relationship status. If you want to be married and everyone else around you is getting married, don't be mad at the world.

If you're walking in jealousy, then you have allowed the opposite of love to penetrate your heart. Now you're looking at circumstances that are causing you to be blind to the truth of God's Word. Why shouldn't we be jealous? The truth is that we have no reason to be jealous, because God has us in His hands. There's no lack or insufficiency with God. Your God, who loves you, provides you with an unlimited supply of blessings and goodness. When you understand that He has already established the best for you, you don't feel a need to be jealous.

When people around you are being blessed and experiencing success, you need to do to them what you would want them to do to you (Luke 6:31). You would want people to congratulate you and celebrate with you, right? If someone gets a brand-new car, stop talking down that person's blessing to make yourself feel good or acting like you don't even see it. Instead, praise God for it! Rejoice!

One of the quickest ways to get rid of jealousy is to do something for the people you're tempted to envy. Go buy them some car freshener for their new car. Buy them a rug for their new house. This will snap jealousy in half and cause that spirit to leave you alone. Otherwise, Satan will try to get into your life and keep you from exemplifying God's love.

Love Does Not Brag

Love doesn't walk around with its chest out, trying to impress people. Love isn't a show-off. It isn't arrogant.

It's important to note that you don't have to put people down to elevate yourself or make yourself feel more important. People are important, and everyone has feelings that can be hurt. We should be aware of how our actions can impact those around us. Instead of bragging, we should esteem others greater than ourselves (Philippians 2:1–4).

> "If you brag, brag of this and this only: That you understand and know me. I'm GOD, and I act in loyal love. I do what's right and set things right and fair, and delight in those who do the same things. These are my trademarks." GOD's Decree.
>
> —*Jeremiah 9:24 (MSG)*

If you boast or brag, it should be about what God has done for you. Use your testimony to inspire someone else to believe in God.

Love Is Not Proud

Love doesn't have a swelled head. In fact, having a swelled head keeps us from loving. It makes us think that we're too good to help someone else. Pride is dangerous because it can make us believe that we're right and everyone else is wrong. It can cause us to justify our actions even when they defy the Word of God.

It's hard to love someone the way God wants us to love when we have a swelled head and are prideful. God wants us to be humble, caring, and giving. Satan is the one who tempts us to be proud, and we have to resist this temptation.

> When pride comes, then comes shame; but with the humble is wisdom.
> —**Proverbs 11:2** (NKJV)

Love Is Not Rude

Love is gentle in its approach to people. God doesn't want us to use our tongues as swords to hurt people. We have a way of making excuses, such as: "This is just who I am. I can't keep my tongue. I'm just direct, and they shouldn't be so sensitive." That's not an attitude of love. Love cares for other people and takes into account how they may be impacted by our actions or words. If you're so direct with people that it comes across as offensive, then you may miss out on opportunities to help them and build them up.

Love Is Not Selfish

It isn't all about you. In church, we are creatures of habit. Most people like to sit in the same seat that they've been sitting in for years. Would it test your love walk to find someone sitting in your usual seat when you get to church? You might think, *"What are you doing here?"* If the person didn't move, would you stare a hole in the back of his or her head through the whole service? Would that little incident derail your whole day?

We should always look to do something for others. How often do you do something for somebody else that has no benefit for you? Everything you do is a seed. An act of kindness grows and spreads, and it may one day come back around to you. On the other hand, if you only care about yourself, that selfishness can turn around and come back to you.

Watch out for selfishness. It can rear its ugly head not only before you decide to show kindness, but also when you're in the midst of an act of kindness or even after the act is complete. Let me give you an example.

One year around Christmas, my daughter decided to do a phenomenal act of kindness. She loves video games. The Bible says that nothing will separate us from the love of God (Romans 8:38–39), but in this case, nothing was going to separate her from her love of video games! (I'm joking, of course.)

On Christmas Eve, she said that she was going to give her Nintendo 3DS to her younger sister. I don't think that she really meant it, but she had an audience of people around her when she said it, including me.

Initially, I believed that she thought she would get something out of it, so I said, "You're saying that you'll give it to your sister? If you really love her and that's your heart's position, then you should do it."

She said, "Okay! I'm going to do it."

"Even if you don't get something you want?" I asked.

Her younger sister overheard the conversation and said, "Dad, I want it now! Can I have it?"

At that point, my older daughter realized what had come out of her mouth, and she started to regret the whole thing. She was irritable and wouldn't eat her food.

I asked her, "What's going on here? Why are you upset?"

She said, "You pressured me!"

"You were giving!" I replied.

When we do good, we need to protect ourselves from getting irritable. Some of us are good to certain people and irritable to everyone else. We are to be kind even to the unlikable people, especially when we don't feel like being kind. For instance, it doesn't please God if you're nice to everybody at work but then come home and lash out at everybody in the house because you're tired of demonstrating kindness.

None of us deserves God's love. It's because of Jesus' obedience to the point of death that we have right standing with God and can enjoy grace and mercy. We need to love others, even if they don't deserve it, because we receive God's love when we don't deserve it.

Love Does Not Get Upset with Others

Love doesn't fly off the handle. It isn't hotheaded. Do you know any hotheads? Their tempers are easily triggered, and you have to walk on eggshells around them. Everything has to be just right, and if it isn't, they might go off. That's not a person who exemplifies love.

Love isn't irritable or easy to offend. If you get offended at everything, you need to work on your love walk. If you're set off by everything someone does, there's something in your heart that isn't right.

> You have heard that it was said, "Love your neighbor and hate your enemies." But I say to you, love your enemies. Pray for those who hurt you.
> —**Matthew 5:43–44** (NCV)

Was something spoken over you when you were a child that you still live with today? Words matter. We often use social media as a place to engage in online wars, but that's not love. Not only are words powerful, but gestures are powerful as well. When people you love roll their eyes at you, that sticks with you.

When we're children, we tend to think that it's the responsibility of adults to come back to us and apologize so we can move on with our lives. If they don't initiate the reconciliation, we won't try to make things right, either. I understand because I've been there, too, but God flipped the script on me. He gave me instructions on how to initiate love toward people when they had never given it to me. God had to show me that instead of waiting on them to do the right thing, I needed to do the right thing first.

Let's not stay where we were last week or last year. Let's grow. Flying off the handle feels good in the moment, but attacking and being hateful toward people, stooping down to Satan's level and using his tactics, isn't our calling or responsibility.

We excuse it and justify ourselves by saying that we'll engage in just one more online battle before we'll pray for the people we're fighting. What we don't realize is that flying off the handle that one time has a ripple effect that harms more than just us and the people we're directly addressing.

Sometimes love is walking away and avoiding the situation. When we walk away, it's not so we can talk negatively about people behind their backs, but so we can take the problem to the Lord and pray for everyone involved. Love requires us to take the high road in conflict, time and time again.

Love Does Not Count Up Wrongs

Love doesn't keep score. If you're walking in love toward others, you're not keeping a tally of their behavior. Stay in your lane. The Bible warns us against focusing on other people's faults:

> *How can you say to your friend, "Let me take that little piece of dust out of your eye"? Look at yourself! You still have that big piece of wood in your own eye. You hypocrite! First,* *take*

the wood out of your own eye. Then you will see clearly to
take the dust out of your friend's eye.
—Matthew 7:4–5 *(NCV)*

Check yourself before you judge someone else. Walking in love doesn't mean that you are now an honorary member of the Facebook police, checking up on everyone and trying to connect the dots. God didn't make you the sin police. We're not supposed to be all up in other people's business.

If love sees something that could be considered compromising, it immediately prays and intercedes for those individuals. The Bible tells us that if someone is in error, we are to restore that person, not point fingers at him or her in condemnation (Galatians 6:1–2).

Think about the woman in the Bible who was caught committing adultery. Jesus didn't condemn her; He condemned the people who brought her to Him (John 8:2–11). That's what love does. Love covers, shields, and protects, *especially* people we don't like.

Love Takes No Pleasure in Evil

This is the kind of fast day I'm after: to break the chains of injustice, get rid of exploitation in the workplace, free the oppressed, cancel debts. What I'm interested in seeing you do is: sharing your food with the hungry, inviting the homeless poor into your homes, putting clothes on the shivering ill-clad, being available to your own families.
—Isaiah 58:6–7 *(MSG)*

Love doesn't revel when others grovel. Love doesn't rejoice in wickedness, injustice, or sin. If something happens that you know isn't right, don't rejoice in it. Love isn't happy when others are humiliated.

Have you ever been a bystander when there was an altercation between two people? Were you one of the cheerleaders egging it on? Maybe you were one of the people fighting, or maybe you saw two people staring each other down, and you were the one to say, "Fight it out!" Instigation is rejoicing in someone else being humiliated. That's not love.

In our society, there are many injustices against different people. God desires for His love to shine through and be the voice of justice, to stand in the gap for the oppressed, to be the voice for the voiceless, to be a helping hand in someone's time of need. This is what love does.

Love Rejoices Over the Truth

Love takes pleasure when truth prevails. The individuals who persecuted Christ weren't interested in the truth. They were upset because Jesus came and taught against their laws and religious doctrines. Even as He sat with them and shared that His mission was to love, their minds were so bent out of shape that the only result they wanted was His death.

They weren't operating in love, because they didn't want to hear the truth. Sometimes we can have our hearts set against somebody. We just want to keep believing what we want about that person. We aren't interested in justice being served; we just want revenge.

Lying, covering something up, and being dishonest are not behaviors consistent with the nature of biblical love.

When we love people, we need to tell them the truth. We often say, "Don't judge me!" when we know that we're doing something wrong, but love doesn't always mean that we have to agree with one another. Let's not be disappointed or angry when people tell us something that we don't want to hear or don't agree with, especially if it's meant to help us, because their honesty shows that they are true friends.

Have you ever had a conversation and later realized when you looked in a mirror that you had something in your nose or your teeth? You probably thought, *"I was sitting in that conversation the whole time, and nobody said anything!"* Love operates in truth—not in a malicious way or to rub it in someone's face, but out of love.

Love Patiently Accepts

Love can put up with just about anything. It has the ability to withstand whatever is thrown at it, and it stands the test of time. This means that if you tell people you love them at the start of your relationship, then six weeks later, twelve weeks later, fifty-two weeks later, you still love them. You're in the trenches with them for however long it takes.

We need to understand that love is something that's given and doesn't look to receive. If you say that you love people but you're only moved by what they do for you, that's not godly love. If you truly love somebody, it doesn't matter if your love isn't reciprocated, because your heart's decision is to love.

Our example, as always, is Christ. God sent His Son when we were all messed up. Even when He was a baby, people went hunting for Him and wanted to kill Him. That was His introduction to the world, even before He was spat upon, whipped beyond human recognition, mocked, and crucified.

This same Jesus, who prayed for His enemies as they were nailing Him to the cross, is the one who told us to love. God gave us His best because He knew that showing us His love would be the example we needed to spread love to other people. We need to endure and keep loving in the face of the messy and hard stuff.

I remember when I first got married. Back then, there was something called the "seven-year itch." People would say that within seven years, you would want to get out. We weren't even close to seven years, but I declared with my own mouth that I wouldn't have a seven-year itch.

Well, the seven years came and went, and I didn't have that itch. Why not? Because I chose not to align my confession with other people's realities or experiences. I also benefited from the wisdom that was given to me before I got married. I knew that marriage would be work. The whole fantasy of riding on a white horse into the sunset on a beach with clear water, every day, is a lie. I took that mental picture and crumpled it up.

Living out the love walk in your day-to-day life requires work. It's work for some of us not to get angry with people. It's work for some of us to put other people ahead of ourselves. It requires work to look at areas in our lives where we need to stretch and grow. Loving unconditionally with biblical love is hard work.

Love Trusts

What does the Word tell us about loving people? If you trust God and somebody lies to you, talks about you, or drags your name through the mud, how does He tell you to respond? Does He tell you to take revenge?

No. He says to "bless those who curse you, and pray for those who spitefully use you" (Luke 6:28 NKJV). As a matter of fact, we're told that if people take something from us, we are to give them something else in addition to what they took (Luke 6:29).

Trusting God means that we live by what God has instituted and instructed us to do. God shares in all of our experiences, and He has declared that we are overcomers. He has also given us instructions for how to love so that we aren't left to figure it out on our own.

Love is ready to believe the best in every person. We don't have one ear on the floor, trying to hear some gossip. Instead, we look for opportunities to give people a chance.

Love jumps in and says, "You know what, guys, let's find out the truth. Let's not talk about people. Let's pray for them."

Do you see a person who is shunned by others? Invite that person to eat with you. You won't do that if you care more about what people think than what God thinks, because you would be putting yourself into a position to be talked about. Trust that God knows best and look for opportunities to love.

Love Always Hopes

Love never looks back. Love always has hope; it never gives up on someone. It's willing to stand in the gap, even if the other person won't meet you halfway.

A great example of this is the prodigal son in the Bible (Luke 15:11–32). The son was impressed with himself and thought that he deserved to be out on his own. He wanted to take his stuff and leave, so the father gave him his inheritance and let him go. When the son realized that he had made a bad decision, he came back home. Who was there, ready to receive him? The father continued to wait for him to return. He never gave up on his son.

That's the love that needs to fill our lives. Some of us can apply this toward family members whom we've grown apart from. Even if they've wandered off or scandalized our name, our love for them remains. When they return, we love them just the same. We shouldn't try to rub things in their faces, saying, "You aren't ever going to see my kids!" That's not the love of God.

Sometimes we're afraid of loving because we're worried that people will take advantage of us, but love frees us from the expectation of getting something in return.

Every time you smile, you're planting a seed. Every time you show kindness instead of offense, you're planting a seed. Every time you choose to move forward instead of living in the wrongs of the past, you're planting a seed. And those seeds will grow and multiply, spreading God's love all over the earth.

Chapter Three Questions

Question: Look at the fifteen characteristics of biblical love as outlined in 1 Corinthians 13:4–7. Which of these characteristics is most apparent in your life or easiest for you to embody? Which of them is least apparent in your life or most difficult for you to embody?

_____

_____

_____

_____

_____

_____

_____

_____

_____

Question: Have you lost connection with someone who used to be in your life? What part did you play in putting distance between you? Are there any practical things you can do to start moving toward reconciliation with that person? Would it be safe for you to reconnect? If so, what is a way you can reach out and show that you are interested in reconnecting and, if needed and possible, reconciling with him or her?

_____

_____

_____

_____

_____

_____

_____

_____

_____

Action: Choose the characteristic of biblical love that is least apparent in your life or the one that you have the greatest struggle applying consistently. Spend some time praying about this area of weakness. Ask God to show you how you can better display this characteristic of love in your life and for Holy Spirit to empower you to do so. Write out a prayer asking Holy Spirit to help you love with the fullness of biblical love and put it up somewhere as a reminder of the love you are called to show to all those around you.

Chapter Three Notes

CONCLUSION

Love Doesn't Quit

We can sing well, tithe consistently, show hospitality, give of our time, pray for people, and be really good at liking certain people, but if we don't have real love, God's kind of love, none of that matters (1 Corinthians 13:1–3). We can pray in tongues all day long, but if our love walk isn't right, none of the rest matters.

Love keeps going until the end. Love doesn't quit or give up. It fights everything that will prevent it from holding its position. Not walking in love sometimes causes us to quit relationships and jobs. Love takes work.

It's not enough to say that you love somebody. If you say that you love someone, you need to show it with the fifteen characteristics of biblical love. Notice that saying, "I love you," isn't one of those biblical ways to show love. Love is a verb and more than just words. When I tell people that I love them, I say, "Don't look at my mouth. Look at my feet."

Anybody can say, "I love you." We throw those words around like trash sometimes, but how many of us actually love our neighbors? How many of us love the person who cuts us off in traffic?

Jesus said, "If you love me, you will obey my commands" (John 14:15 NCV). None of us would come out and say that we don't love God, but He says that if we love Him, we need to do what He says. Love is not optional:

> *If anyone boasts, "I love God," and goes right on hating his brother or sister, thinking nothing of it, he is a liar. If he won't love the person he can see, how can he love the God he can't see? The command we have from Christ is blunt: Loving God includes loving people. You've got to love both.*
> *—1 John 4:20–21 (MSG)*

Loving God includes loving people. You have to do both. If you're saying that you love God but you're not loving people, then you don't really love God. Your love is fake. If we aren't loving people the way we're supposed to love them, then we don't truly want God's will and everything He has for us. The body of Christ has to be the one place where people can come and feel the love of God—not only within the four walls of a church, but in all of our day-to-day interactions. Everyone we encounter should experience God's love.

Loving somebody is not a once-in-a-lifetime occurrence; it's a constant and continuous walk. In the places where our love is the weakest, let's continue to press in and grow. When we find ourselves frustrated, let's not give in and fly off the handle, but rather see it as an opportunity to become more patient. When we're tempted to point fingers and call out others as being fake, let's look closely at ourselves and remember that our first responsibility is to look in the mirror. Real love starts with us, and it can and will change the world.

REFERENCES

Notes

1. Lewis, Clive Staples. *The Four Loves*. Harcourt Brace Jovanovich, 1991.

2. *Merriam-Webster*, "jealous." https://www.merriam-webster.com/dictionary/jealous.

3. *Merriam-Webster*, "fake." https://www.merriam-webster.com/dictionary/fake.

4. *Lexico*, "patience." https://www.lexico.com/definition/patience.

About the Author

Dr. LaMarcus A. Keys is the founder and pastor of Life of Victory Worship Center, which is located in Oxnard, California (est. 2009). Dr. Keys had a strong call upon his life as a young child. He began ministering at the age of 14 in his hometown of Dallas, Texas, and he never swayed from his calling. Dr. Keys was first licensed at the young age of 14, and he was later licensed at the age of 18 by his father, Apostle Urban Brown of Life in Christ Family Church in Lancaster, Texas.

Prior to launching Life of Victory Worship Center, Dr. Keys served for over eight years with Dr. Tom Pickens at Antelope Valley Christian Center in Lancaster,

California. He was licensed under this ministry in the early 2000s by Dr. Pickens and was ordained in 2008.

Dr. Keys's motto concerning ministry is simple: "Teach the Word, Live the Word, and Love the people." One of his assignments to the body of Christ is to minister on faith, unity, and love. His desire is to see all believers full of faith and belief, fulfilling God's intended purpose for their lives, and living the life of victory that God has promised through His Word.

Dr. Keys is a graduate of Rhema Bible Training College, and of Oxnard College with an emphasis on television broadcasting and production. He received an honorary Doctor of Divinity degree from St. Thomas in 2016. He has been the recipient of countless leadership and ministry awards, including Ventura County's 2014 NAACP Community Pastor's Award.

Dr. Keys is a businessman, entrepreneur, public speaker, and trainer with over twenty years of experience in the field of television broadcasting and production, over twenty-two years of management experience, and over thirty years in ministry. He continues to develop leadership programs and tools that are designed to take every leader to his or her next level of success.

Dr. Keys's first passion is his family. He has been happily married to his wife, First Lady Danielle Keys, for twenty-three years, and together they are the blessed parents of three daughters—Jasmine, Jada, and Jordyn—whom he affectionately refers to as his "angels."

Made in the USA
Middletown, DE
06 November 2021

51275224R00046